Original title:
Dark Matter Ditties

Copyright © 2025 Creative Arts Management OÜ
All rights reserved.

Author: Aidan Marlowe
ISBN HARDBACK: 978-1-80567-824-3
ISBN PAPERBACK: 978-1-80567-945-5

Lunar Nocturnes

A moonbeam slipped on banana peels,
Chasing stars, spinning cosmic wheels.
Cats in spacesuits dance and prance,
While aliens plot an intergalactic romance.

Twirling comets with wobbling tails,
Nibbling on jelly, ignoring the scales.
Asteroids bounce like rubber balls,
Singing songs in echoing halls.

Galactic Daydreams

In a nebula, I lost my socks,
Floating free like some cosmic rocks.
Space cows graze on stardust hay,
Mooing softly in a zero-grav way.

Teleporting to Mars for a fizzy drink,
Juggling planets with a side of pink.
Martians giggle, spill their tea,
As Venus hides behind a laughing spree.

Emptiness in Resonance

Echoes of nothing fill the void,
Bouncing off thoughts that can't be avoid.
Chuckling while bouncing on the moon,
A kazoo serenade, oh what a tune!

Bubbles of laughter in the blackest night,
Worms in tuxedos getting ready for flight.
Hovering tables, all set to dine,
Where cosmic chefs mix soup and wine.

Harmonies of the Black

Whispers in nothing, oh what a clap,
A cosmic concert with a twisty map.
Laughing black holes throw a grand bash,
Inviting the stars for a space-time splash.

Jokes fly like meteors in a twirl,
While quasars spin, giving gravity a whirl.
In the silence, the giggles ignite,
As voids dance in the shimmering night.

Celestial Secrets

Stars in the sky, they blink and they wink,
Planets collide, while space takes a drink.
Black holes that giggle, do you hear their roar?
Physics is silly, who needs to explore?

Aliens drop by, they bring their own snacks,
Telling us jokes while we stare at their backs.
With telescopes pointed, we watch with delight,
Cosmic comedians, putting on a light.

Elusive Cosmic Chords

The universe hums a mysterious tune,
Made up of echoes from way past June.
Guitars in the void, played by stars so bright,
Strumming the notes in the dead of the night.

What if we danced on the rings of a moon?
Jiving with comets and singing a rune.
The rhythm of space, a universal groove,
Bopping through stardust, we start to move.

Obscured Tunes of Infinity

Galaxy whispers, they tease me so clear,
A tune from a far star, oh what do I hear?
Jokes played in silence, by neutron and quark,
Laughter in shadows, igniting the dark.

Cosmic mishaps, like socks that don't match,
Quasars debate, should we catch or just hatch?
Through chaos and mystery, I strum a bright jive,
Singing with the splendor of all things alive.

The Sound of Nothingness

In the silence of space, there's a giggle I chase,
Nothingness chuckles, not leaving a trace.
Whispers of quarks play hide and seek,
While galaxies dance, both dizzy and meek.

A vacuum of funny, with zero to show,
But oh how it tickles when nothing can grow!
In a cosmos of jest, where laughter takes flight,
Not even a sound, yet it feels so right.

Fragments of Forgotten Galaxies

In a vacuum of space, things went awry,
Stardust sneezed, and oh my, oh my!
A comet slipped on a banana peel,
While aliens danced, with a wobbly wheel.

Planets giggled, caught in a whirl,
As moons spun around in a dizzy twirl.
Lost in the silence, a joke took flight,
Twinkling starlights shared laughter at night.

Tales from the Event Horizon

A black hole sighed with a grunt and a creak,
It tried to charm, but its jokes went bleak.
Space-time folded like an origami swan,
Leaving behind just a giggle and yawn.

At the edge, where chaos reigns supreme,
Asteroids plotted to steal the scene.
With a wink and a nudge, they spun round and around,
In a cosmic circus, hilarity found.

The Dark Between Stars

In the ink between stars, a punster resides,
Telling tales of quirks where humor abides.
A neutron danced in a tutu so bright,
While photons tickled the waves of the night.

Blackness chuckled at the giggling glitch,
As wormholes twisted like a playful witch.
With a cosmic chuckle, they spun out their quips,
While galaxies plotted their interstellar trips.

Subtle Shadows

Under shadows so subtle, a joke comes alive,
Where quasars quibble and spacetime takes a dive.
Jupiters barrel rolled in a game of tag,
While silly starlings dressed up in a rag.

Nebulas whispered secrets of folly and fun,
As they danced in sync with the light of the sun.
Invisible laughs, they softly blast,
Creating a ruckus while drifting so fast.

Celestial Murmurs

In the cosmos, jokes collide,
Like stars that twinkle and slide.
Planets whisper, make a jest,
Even black holes need a rest.

The comets zoom with speed so grand,
While aliens play in a rubber band.
Wormholes laugh in a curvy way,
As galaxies dance on a cosmic day.

Shooting stars sip on stardust tea,
Wondering if they're really free.
Meteorites drop with a wink,
Spilling secrets in twilight pink.

Gravity trips with a silly fall,
Stellar giggles echo through all.
With every comical cosmic scene,
The universe joins in, so serene.

Bittersweet Void

In a vacuum, silence reigns,
But funny thoughts stay in chains.
Floating jokes that drift and sway,
A twist of fate in the Milky Way.

Nebulas wear their fluffiest hair,
While eclipses play hide and seek with flair.
The cosmos teases with a grin,
As space-time giggles deep within.

Asteroids toss a punchline around,
While supernovae burst with a sound.
In the void, where strange things dwell,
Every empty space tells a tale so well.

Quasars wink with their brightest light,
As cosmic clowns take flight at night.
With laughter echoing through the gloom,
The universe blooms in its funny room.

The Unseen Symphony

In the realm where shadows drift,
A symphony of giggles is swift.
Toneless harmonies laugh in glee,
As spirits dance in a waltzing spree.

Planets hum their silly tunes,
While starlit marionettes play spoons.
The rhythm bounces off of dark,
Creating laughter without a spark.

Comedic concepts swirl in space,
Jovial jesters leave their trace.
Harmony rings in the voids that sway,
As the unseen music leads the way.

Galactic choirs sing of fun,
While cosmic pranks have just begun.
With every note that spirals high,
The unseen symphony winks at the sky.

Celestial Echoes

Echoes drift on cosmic breeze,
Joking around like a swarm of bees.
Stars chuckle in a playful tease,
In the galaxy's whimsical keys.

Black holes snicker, pulling tight,
As stardust dances, a sheer delight.
Astrophysics plays hide-and-seek,
While supernova bursts find the meek.

The cosmos plays its merry game,
As laughter sparkles, never tame.
Echoing through the astral haze,
A comedic tune in bright displays.

Reaching far, the fun won't cease,
In the universe, we find our peace.
Cosmic quips and merry calls,
In celestial echoes, joy enthralls.

Mysteries Unraveled

Floating in space, what a sight,
A pancake planet? That's just a fright!
Aliens giggle, their jokes quite absurd,
While comets zoom past, totally unheard.

Starlight winks, what a tease,
A cosmic game of hide and freeze!
Quasars dance, doing the twist,
Who knew the universe had such a list?

Stellar Soliloquy

Shooting stars might need a map,
For every time they take a nap!
Galaxies spin with socks askew,
Wormholes giggle, 'Hey, what's new?'

The Moon's got jokes, a real wise guy,
Says Mars is just a little shy.
When Saturn rings in a funky tone,
It's disco night, let's all moan!

Whispers from the Cosmos

Cosmic winds whisper soft and low,
'Did you hear that? Oh, no! Oh, no!'
Asteroids chuckle, their paths all err,
'Oops! I did it again, I swear!'

Zodiac signs having tea in space,
Leo spilled his drink all over the place!
Virgo's cleaning, with quite the fuss,
'Can someone help? It's a cosmic mess!'

Chasing the Dark

Chasing shadows, the stars say boo,
Black holes hiding, what will they do?
With a wink and a nod, they play peek-a-boo,
While tiny moons giggle, oh who knew?

Nebulas bloom in colors so bright,
'Let's throw a rave, it's party night!'
But watch out for gravity, sneaky and sly,
It might bring you down if you fly too high!

The Veil of Existence

In shadows where the quirks reside,
Glitches dance with cosmic pride.
Got lost in a neutron's jig,
Forgot how to pull that cosmic twig.

Beneath the stars, a giggle beams,
While planets plot their secret schemes.
A black hole's wink, a star's shy blush,
Oops! There goes another galactic hush.

Haunting in the Heavens

A ghostly comet trails behind,
Playing tag with space and time.
The Milky Way shakes with laughter,
Who knew the night had such a crafter?

With every twinkle, a joke is made,
While meteors softly serenade.
Aliens chuckle, peeking out,
"Did you hear the one about the clout?"

Lament of the Spacetime

Time's a trickster, never still,
Poking fun, it bends at will.
"Move faster!" shouts that pesky clock,
While I just sit and eat my rock.

Einstein's hair has stories to tell,
Of cosmic pranks and gravity's spell.
Warping thoughts, through spirals they fly,
Is that a wormhole? Oh my, oh my!

Secrets of Silent Spheres

Planets whisper in hushed tones,
Trading jokes through orbital zones.
Gravity pulls a prank or two,
"Hey Earth, catch the moon – boo-hoo!"

Saturn laughs with rings so wide,
While the stars roll over, side by side.
Each twinkling orb has tales to spin,
"Join our dance, let the fun begin!"

Echoes of a Void

In the vastness, whispers play,
Mysterious voices having their say.
They giggle and laugh, quite the game,
In the nothingness, who's to blame?

With each echo, a riddle found,
Spinning tales without a sound.
No one knows where they come from,
But try to catch them, oh what fun!

Floating thoughts, like bubbles burst,
Carried by winds of cosmic thirst.
In this emptiness, jokes abound,
Where logic swirls, and craziness is crowned.

Lost in a dance of utter grace,
These echoes jump from place to place.
A comedy show without a stage,
Casting laughter across the age.

Starlit Secrets

Twinkling lights with tales to share,
A secret club in endless air.
Cosmic confessions, sly and bright,
Giggles echo through the night.

Stars gossip about human quirks,
How we fumble, and do our jerks.
"Did you see that?" they snicker away,
As comets crash in a playful fray.

In the night, no rules apply,
Galaxies wink as they pass by.
The humor hides in a cosmic twist,
A laughter-fueled, celestial mist.

With every twinkle, secrets unfold,
Jokes of the universe, brave and bold.
So join the gathering, gaze alight,
And laugh along with stars so bright.

The Enigma of Invisible Threads

Tangled lines that weave the unknown,
Invisible threads are all but shown.
They play hide and seek in cosmic light,
Tugging softly, causing delight.

What holds the planets in their place?
A prankster god with a chuckling face?
He pulls at strings with a wink, you see,
And all of space giggles in glee.

Yesterday's theories, flimsy as lace,
Love to trip over in their chase.
While quantum jokes fly through the air,
Entangled humor is everywhere.

So let us ponder the cosmic jest,
In this grand puzzle, we're but guests.
Pull a thread, see what's revealed,
In the laughter, the truth is sealed.

Cosmic Rhythms

Planets dance to a silent beat,
In orbits round, they sway on their feet.
Gravity's pull, a cha-cha slide,
As stardust shimmies, laughs collide.

Galaxies spin, a whimsical twirl,
They swirl and giggle, a cosmic whirl.
Each rotation, a punchline to tell,
In the universe's grand carousel.

Black holes laugh, they gobble whole,
While neutron stars play hide-and-seek role.
In this rhythm, joy's found anew,
Stellar jokes echo, me and you.

So join the dance, let spirits soar,
Through the vast cosmos, forever explore.
In twinkling beats, our hearts align,
For what is space but a jest divine?

The Fractal of Darkness

In shadows where the lost socks roam,
A cosmic dance in the laundry foam.
Each twist and turn a hidden plot,
The universe giggles at what we've got.

Chaos spins in a spaghettified way,
While dust bunnies sing and frolic and play.
The galaxies swirl, oh what a sight,
As we search for our keys under couch light.

Fractals form in the night sky's weave,
Supernova shimmers as planets conceive.
But tell me, dear friend, what's that on your shoe?
A piece of the cosmos? Or last week's stew?

So raise a glass to the strange and absurd,
To the laughter in places we've never heard.
For even in darkness, humor won't hide,
In the vast universe, let chuckles collide.

Harmonics of the Beyond

In the depth of space, where the echoes play,
Aliens hum in a wobbly sway.
A chorus of quarks dance in a line,
While space cows moo in a syncopate rhyme.

The stars all giggle, twinkle with glee,
As black holes slurp in a cosmic spree.
Frequencies rise from the depths below,
In a symphony where we all steal the show.

Wormholes whisper in waffle cone tones,
As galaxy squirrels throw acorns and bones.
Sound waves travel, a funky display,
As echoes giggle at night and by day.

Let's jive with the comets, groove with the moons,
And laugh as we twirl to the cosmic tunes.
In the emptiness, find a beat to sing,
For harmonics of beyond are a magical thing.

The Hidden Horizon

Behind the skyline, where shadows converge,
Lies a festival where oddities emerge.
Horizon giggles, peeking around,
While we search for lost worlds under the ground.

The clouds play peek-a-boo with the sun,
As rainbows tickle, making a run.
Mystery sprouts from invisible seeds,
As laughter unfurls like wild dandelion weeds.

The edge of sight holds realms anew,
Banana-shaped planets pass right on through.
At sunrise, the horizon gives a wink,
As we sip our coffee and ponder, don't think!

So here's to the things we can't quite see,
The jests of the cosmos, wild and free.
For every corner turned holds a new surprise,
In the hidden horizon, we learn to rise.

Veils of the Unseen

In a clubhouse hidden beyond the scope,
Ghosts crack jokes, wrapped in the rope.
With veils of laughter and playful sighs,
They dance around, much to our surprise.

The universe teases with shades of disguise,
Like cats in boxes, a grand surprise.
Invisible realms where humor resides,
In the unseen corners, joy abides.

So pull back the curtain, take a quick glance,
The uninvited quips make us dance.
A giggle erupts from the space in between,
As we ponder the veils that are rarely seen.

In the cloak of twilight, where spirits convene,
Humor's the language, and laughter's the theme.
So let's toast to the unseen with cheer,
For in every shadow, the funny is near.

The Forgotten Frequencies

In the void where giggles play,
Lost waves dance, then run away.
A signal from a cosmic cat,
Meowing soft in this vast expat.

With tunes of chaos, they hum and blink,
Space-time's joke, a cosmic wink.
The echoes twist with silly grace,
As comets trip in a dance-off space.

Ghostly voices on the line,
Making fun of space's design.
Interstellar jesters flip and tease,
Tickling stars with cosmic ease.

So tune your ears to giddy sounds,
A front-row seat where laughter bounds.
In shadows deep, surprises soar,
Forgotten freqs forevermore.

Whispered Phantoms

In the corner where whispers creep,
Phantom giggles dance, not sleep.
In the fridge, they hide and snack,
Nibbling on the midnight crack.

Floating high with a silly cheer,
Boo! A chuckle from a chandelier.
They tumble down, like marbles spun,
Spooking cats while having fun.

They paint the walls with shadowed jest,
Making mischief, never rest.
With a swirl and twirl, they'd steal the show,
Winking at us from the below.

So if you hear a soft little peep,
Don't be scared, they're not here to weep.
Just playful whispers in the night,
Bringing giggles, oh what a fright!

Beyond the Brink

At the edge of space, a funny sight,
Aliens laughing in cosmic delight.
Riding waves of inflatable dreams,
Bouncing high on starlit beams.

They've got jokes about the Earth,
Stealing secrets of our worth.
A tickle fight with comets bright,
Giggling past in a splash of light.

Beyond the brink of laughter's realm,
They captain ships with a rubber helm.
With zany hats, they caper and tease,
While spiraling past with the greatest of ease.

So join the fun, let worries sink,
Out here, the stars always wink.
In the void where chuckles ring,
Life's a joke, let giggles cling.

Specters of the Sky

Up above, the specters glide,
With silly grins, they oft confide.
In clouds of foam, they float and spin,
Tickling stars, oh where to begin?

They hover near and drop a pun,
Creating shadows that twirl and run.
Every star a glimmering face,
In joy's embrace, they find their place.

With cosmic giggles and silly pranks,
They color space with glowing flanks.
In this mirthful sight of glee,
The universe is wild and free.

So when you gaze at the night so vast,
Remember those giggles, shadows cast.
Specters of the sky, up high they play,
Spreading laughter, come what may.

Celestial Conundrums

In the void where stars play hide and seek,
Galaxies giggle, yet they never speak.
Planets spin tales of cosmic delight,
While comets tease with a wink of bright.

Aliens ponder the purpose of socks,
Hiding their treasures in interstellar blocks.
With a wink and a grin, they bring forth glee,
In a universe full of playful debris.

Light-years stretch like a cat on the floor,
As black holes snicker, always wanting more.
Gravity pulls at our curious toes,
While shooting stars giggle as they strike their pose.

So let's laugh at space's curious ways,
Where celestial wonders put us in a daze.
The universe plays, with us its guest,
In this cosmic circus, we jest with zest.

The Dance of the Unobserved

In shadows where the unseen twirl,
A galaxy of giggles begins to unfurl.
Invisible forces throw a grand ball,
With whispers of chaos that tickle us all.

Silly strings pull on everything near,
Cheeking physics, they chuckle and cheer.
While neutrinos prance, no one can see,
Making a ruckus as they skip with glee.

Quasars flash secrets in colors so bold,
Yet no one can touch what can't be sold.
Space-time jives in a wobbly beat,
Leaving us laughing, our minds incomplete.

So join in the fun with a wink and a glance,
As particles join in a quirky dance.
In the realms where the unseen roam free,
The universe giggles and dances with glee.

Between Light and Nothing

In the space where shadows chat and prance,
Lies a riddle wrapped in a mischievous dance.
The flicker of light plays peekaboo games,
While nothingness chuckles, feeling no shame.

A photon trips and lands in a blink,
Wonders if dark could be lighter than ink.
Amidst the giggles of unseen affairs,
Waves and particles swap silly stares.

Cosmic jokes float in a vast friendly void,
Where silent chuckles swirl, oh so coy.
Between here and there, what could it be?
The laughter of stars spills over with glee.

So ponder the gaps with a jest in your heart,
In realms of the unseen, we all play a part.
With a grin on the edge of the cosmic expanse,
Each moment alights in a whimsical dance.

Wandering in the Blackness

Lost in the void, I take a stroll,
Where absence giggles and wonders unfold.
Stars are the campfire in this endless night,
While humor ignites in the absence of light.

Through the black, I see shadows that sway,
Grinning at planets both quirky and gray.
Where silence is loud and laughter is free,
In this cosmic café, we sip on the glee.

Oddities thrive in the dark's embrace,
Where quarks make mischief, a funny little race.
The universe jeers as it spins 'round and 'round,
With jokesters galore in this vast playground.

So here's to the voyage through shadows and light,
To the fun that we find in the dark of the night.
For amidst all the chaos and playful affairs,
It's the laughter in nothing that truly unpairs.

Whispers Beyond the Light.

In galaxies far, they giggle and sway,
Invisible friends, who love to play.
They tickle the stars, a cosmic delight,
Twinkling and teasing beyond the twilight.

A comet once said, with a wink and a grin,
"I'm faster than light, can you believe that sin?"
The planets just chuckled, in orbits so neat,
As they joined in the laughter, all light on their feet.

A black hole yawned, with a sight so grand,
"I suck in all things, isn't that just bland?"
Yet in its dark heart, a joke did reside,
"Why don't stars visit? Too much dark inside!"

So if you look up, and you hear a soft sigh,
Know it's the cosmos, just passing by.
With whispers and giggles from beyond our view,
Making mischief in ways we never knew!

Celestial Whispers

In the cold void, where silence reigns,
A meteor quips, while bending its chains.
"What did the star say to the wandering comet?"
"You're out of this world, and I dig your outfit!"

In twilight's embrace, the cosmos collide,
With laughter and tales, they can't seem to hide.
A nebula chuckles, enshrouded in mist,
"I'm just full of gas, but I still gotta exist!"

Old Saturn spun round, with rings all aglow,
He danced to a tune only he seemed to know.
"Ever seen a planet do the cha-cha slide?"
With a flick of a ring, he took joyride!

Through the vastness, bright giggles can bloom,
In the heart of the cosmos, there's always more room.
For echoes of laughter, both near and afar,
Celestial whispers, the true shining stars.

The Silence of Nebulae

In nebulae's hush, secrets do seep,
Like cosmic gossip, that's yours to keep.
A starlet once whispered, 'I'm just a great ball!'
While spinning her dreams, she was having a ball!

Oh, the dark skies roll with celestial jokes,
Where asteroids chuckle and wormholes poke.
"Why'd the rover cross the moon's side?"
"To see the other crater, for a joyride!"

Galaxies twirl in a whimsical race,
With bright shooting stars that always keep pace.
A supernova said, with a deliberate flare,
"I blow up the night like I just don't care!"

The silence is rich with a cosmic delight,
Where laughter and stardust shimmer at night.
In shadows of dust, where the noggins can roam,
The nebula giggles, calling space its home!

Shadows in the Cosmic Dance

In shadows that twirl, the cosmos do sway,
Dancing with rhythm, they brighten the gray.
"Why was the quasar so ready to twine?"
"It had too much energy—couldn't keep in line!"

Around the great void where echoes are caught,
Stars strut their stuff, giving all they have sought.
A dwarf planet stomped, with a wink and a cheer,
"I may be small, but I'm loud and I'm here!"

Pulsars thrummed tunes, like a galactic band,
As gravity clapped with an unseen hand.
"Let's make a ruckus in this silence so stark,
We'll light up the heavens with our cosmic spark!"

So if you look closer at the night's grand parade,
You'll see the shadows that dance unafraid.
For the universe spins with mirth and great zest,
In the shadows of stars, we're all highly blessed!

Embracing the Unknown

In the void where wonders hide,
Einstein grins—let logic slide.
Space is silly, can't you see?
Wobbling stars sip cosmic tea.

Galaxies whirl like dance hall floors,
Neutron stars slam—open doors!
Aliens chuckle, "Hey, it's cool!"
What's a spaceship without a school?

Black holes eat all the homework, too,
"Oops, my project is overdue!"
Asteroids roll, a wobbly trot,
In the cosmos, we've got a lot!

So here's to mysteries all around,
In the universe, laughter's found!
Let's toss our fears with a quirky spin,
And dance with the stars—let the fun begin!

Interstellar Melancholy

Beyond the stars of happy dreams,
Floating thoughts like silent screams.
Planets sigh in cosmic woe,
While comets joke, "Don't take it slow!"

Galactic giggles, laughter spreads,
While vacuum hums through emptiness.
Neptune grumbles in shades of blue,
But a red dwarf twirls a hula too!

Astronauts miss their favorite pie,
In zero G, it floats on by!
Sadness echoes in the skies,
Yet shooting stars bring silly highs.

So as we drift through endless night,
Let's find the joy in our own plight.
For every frown, there's laughter near,
Cosmic chaos brings good cheer!

Cosmic Shadows

In the corners of the cosmos wide,
Shadows play and secrets bide.
Moonbeams dance with funky flair,
While black holes giggle—"Do we dare?"

Stars are jesters, twinkling bright,
Yodeling tunes in the deep dark night.
Gravity pulls, but who can tell,
If it's a fall or a merry swell?

Space-time tickles, what a ride!
Around each bend, a secret hides.
Astrology scribbles silly charts,
Mapping laughs across the stars!

So when the shadows start to creep,
Remember the giggles in the deep.
In every void, a spark can glow,
Laughter's the light we all should know!

Dreaming in the Dark

Floating dreams on cosmic streams,
Wishful thoughts burst at the seams.
Nebulas swirl in vibrant hues,
While galaxies whisper silly news.

Stardust blankets the night's embrace,
While twilight gives a cheeky face.
"Close your eyes, let's take a trip,"
Says the universe with a gentle flip!

Backyard telescopes, wishes made,
Aliens toast, no need to fade!
In the quiet, giggles arise,
As dreams unfurl to starry skies.

So let's drift on a cosmic spree,
With laughter soaring wild and free.
In the dark, let's dance and play,
Until the dawn steals night away!

The Geometry of the Invisible

In shadows where the odd shapes play,
A triangle winks, then runs away.
Circles giggle, square does frown,
Who knew math could clown around?

Lines of laughter twist and curve,
With angles sharp, they deftly swerve.
Pythagoras, with cheeky grin,
Says all the fun's where it begins.

Paradoxes dodge and weave,
Chasing points that won't believe.
Invisible forces, pulling tight,
Make geometry a silly sight.

Laughing at dimensions missed,
Funny shapes, you can't resist.
So come and play in this delight,
Where math is always out of sight.

Shades of the Universe

In hues of laughter, colors blend,
Nebulas flaunt, with giggles, they send.
A cosmic dance in pastel light,
Stars throw confetti, oh, what a sight!

Reddish giggles, blue whispers too,
Galaxies tease, saying boo-hoo!
Shooting stars, like pranks on high,
Painted skies just love to fly.

The universe plays peek-a-boo,
With comets dressed in vibrant hue.
Planets spin in a merry chase,
Each shade a joke in endless space.

In this spectrum, fun does swell,
A canvas where the strange do dwell.
So grab a star, make a wish bright,
Join the shades in cosmic delight.

Navigating the Night

Wandering stars with maps askew,
Guide me through the night, will you?
A compass giggles, spinning fast,
As shadows shiver, and fates are cast.

Moonbeams whisper secrets sweet,
While night critters shuffle their feet.
I bump into space, what a blunder!
A nebula laughs, breaks the thunder.

With every twist and turn I take,
The universe laughs, for fun's at stake.
Navigating cosmic delight,
With laughter bright in the heart of night.

Stars play tag, planets have fun,
Chasing my dreams 'til night is done.
Through the galaxy, I roam and bounce,
In darkness, joy, and light, I pounce.

Eclipsed Moments

When the sun plays peekaboo,
The moon joins in the fun, too!
Shadows giggle, time stands still,
As light and dark dance at will.

What's an eclipse, but nature's jest?
A cosmic trick, it's truly the best!
Sun wearing the moon as a hat,
While stars shake hands, and cats chase rat.

In these fleeting, funny affairs,
Moments lost in cosmic glares.
With each eclipse, the universe grins,
A playful game, where laughter spins.

So wave at the stars, give a cheer,
For eclipsed times we hold so dear.
With every darkened, joyous smile,
Life's eclipses are well worth the while.

Unraveling the Unknown

In the cosmos, a dance with a wink,
Particles giggle, or so we think.
Gravity trips on a cosmic joke,
While stars tease light, or so they poke.

Wormholes are portals, a flip and a spin,
Time forgot how to even begin.
Quarks wear hats, but why wear a tie?
The universe laughs, oh me, oh my!

Galaxies swirl like a party at night,
Spinning and twirling, oh what a sight!
They toast to the void with glasses of air,
And joke about things that aren't really there.

With friends made of nothing, they cheer and collide,
In a frolicsome dance where no one can hide.
What's real in the cosmos? Who even can tell?
Just laughter and whispers—oh, we know them well.

Shadowed Veils

Under a blanket of shadows so deep,
Mysteries gather, no need for sleep.
A riddle of smiles with a twist and a turn,
In veils of the dark, there's much to learn.

Ghosts of lost thoughts waltz through the void,
Tickling our brains, like children overjoyed.
A cosmos where silliness rules the day,
With laughter echoing, come join the play!

Whispers of nonsense drift in the breeze,
They tickle our senses with cosmic tease.
A universe giggles, while shadows all sway,
In a world where the silly takes charge of the play.

So come take a peek where the shadows convene,
Join in the fun, be silly and keen.
In a realm full of nothing, who knows what you'll find?
Just shadows and giggles, and laughter entwined!

The Beauty of Nothingness

In the void where all things seem to hide,
A beauty blooms wide, nowhere to bide.
Absence of matter, yet fullness of cheer,
The elegance of emptiness is oh-so-clear.

Naughtiness dances in the seams of the night,
As nothingness sparkles, a curious sight.
With a wink and a nudge, it plays all around,
Creating a wonder where laughter is found.

A parade of nonsense skips through the air,
In a land full of nothing, we float without care.
Balloons made of stardust drift easy and light,
In the beauty of absence, there's joy in our flight.

So revel in nothing, embrace the absurd,
Silly thoughts tumble, unheard and unstirred.
In this grand choreography, we twirl and we spin,
Cherishing the moments, where humor begins.

Light Without Form

A beam with no body, it jumps and it plays,
Dancing through shadows in whimsical ways.
It chuckles with colors that shimmer and glide,
Light without form, what a fabulous ride!

In a realm of the quirky, it flits as it glows,
With flashes of laughter, nobody knows.
It leaps from the clouds, a sprightly delight,
Painting the heavens, a canvas so bright.

This luminary jester, it twirls in the dark,
Finding a giggle in every small spark.
It teases the void like a playful spirit,
Filling the night with a laughter we hear it.

A lighthearted prankster, forever it roams,
Through spaces undulating, it makes its own homes.
With flashes of mischief, it paints on the sky,
In the brightness of nothing, we dance and we fly!

Phantom Light

In the corner, shadows play,
Whispers of a wily ray.
A giggle from a twinkling star,
Chasing shadows from afar.

Invisible gems in the night,
Wobbling in a comical flight.
A dance with no one else's eyes,
Mixing laughter in the skies.

Echoed in the Void

Bouncing jokes from light years back,
In the space between the crack.
Did you hear the vacuum's sigh?
Or was that just a comet's lie?

A chuckle floats in stellar winds,
Where time and humor twist and spin.
It's a riddle that flies pretty high,
Tickling thoughts as planets cry.

Cosmic Lullabies

Singing softly to the night,
With giggles wrapped in starlight.
Planets hum an old delight,
While the comets take their flight.

A lull in space, a cosmic glee,
As the cosmos counts to three.
In the cradle of stars so bright,
Celestial dreams take their flight.

The Symmetry of Silence

Quiet jokes in a stark embrace,
Where echoes giggle with grace.
A stillness wrapped in humor's cloak,
As laughter's shadows gently poke.

In the void where whispers sneak,
A cosmic chuckle starts to peak.
The symmetry of silence sings,
With playful tales from hidden things.

Ethereal Dreams

In shadows where the giggles hide,
A cosmic dance, a silly ride.
Nebulae laugh and comets play,
In a waltz of night turning to day.

Unicorns and aliens, side by side,
Bumping into moons, oh what a glide!
Jellyfish floating like wobbly dreams,
Joking with stars in spiraled beams.

Planets caper with glittery trails,
As spacemen tell their ghostly tales.
There's humor in the weight of the void,
Where the real and surreal coexist, overjoyed.

Ethereal laughter fills the air,
As we waltz with whims without a care.
In the realm where dreams ignite,
Everything's funny in the soft starlight.

Whispers of the Time Warp

A tick and a tock, then a spin and a twirl,
In a time warp where oddities swirl.
Socks and shoes fly, oh what a sight,
As seconds get tangled during the night.

Wormholes giggle as they twist and bend,
While clocks and calendars pretend to mend.
Echoes of laughter ripple through space,
Following shadows in a cosmic chase.

Past and future having a tea,
Whispering secrets about you and me.
As timelines hiccup in a joyous fit,
The universe chuckles, never to quit.

Time wobbles like jelly in a jar,
Tickling the edges of every star.
It's a comical romp through the fabric of fate,
Where laughter loops, oh isn't it great?

Notes from a Fading Star

Once a bright spark in the vast, vast sea,
Now scribbles and doodles, just let it be.
A twinkle that fumbled, a giggle that flared,
Gets stuck in a black hole, suddenly scared.

Messages faded like a piece of cheese,
Texting the cosmos with thoughts that tease.
"I'm still shining, just in a new form,"
Chortles the star as it begins to transform.

A pop and a crackle, celestial glee,
Whispers of nonsense, feel free to flee!
Chasing a comet, oh what a spree,
While nebulae blush amid laughter and glee.

Notes from that star, once mighty and bright,
Now scribbles that make us giggle at night.
In every glow where the shadows dance,
Is a joke of the cosmos, just give it a chance.

Flickers of the Unknown

In the places where shadows play,
Flickers of mystery brighten the day.
A wiggly wisp makes a curious sound,
As it wiggles and jives all around.

Things that are fuzzy and things that are clear,
Dance in the ether, bringing us cheer.
A puff of oddness blooms like a flower,
In the hilarious grip of an unseen power.

Particles giggle, colliding in jest,
Creating a ruckus at the cosmic fest.
Behind every flickering starry glare,
Is a chuckle waiting, light as the air.

So join in the jive, in the wink of the eye,
And celebrate wonders that zoom and fly.
For in the unknown, laughter will sprout,
With every flicker, new smiles come out.

The Melancholy of the Infinite

A sock lost in the void, oh dear,
The laundry sings a cosmic cheer.
Stars laugh as they spin and twirl,
While my shoe's lost in a galactic whirl.

I ponder the fate of my other sock,
A cosmic mystery, a ticking clock.
Did it find a planet, all fresh and bright?
Or is it stuck in a black hole's night?

Leprechauns dance in the nebulous haze,
Chasing dust bunnies in a spiral maze.
With each twinkle, they giggle and play,
While my couch devours my socks every day.

Oh, the universe spins with socks in hand,
In this fabric of fate, we make our stand.
So, let laughter echo, let the cosmos applaud,
For every sock lost is a tale quite odd.

Driftwood in the Cosmos

A piece of driftwood on the Milky Way,
Wishing to join in the grand ballet.
It nods to the stars, a cosmic boat,
While the sun raises juice in a celestial tote.

It drifts past planets, all shiny and bright,
Waving at comets that race in delight.
"Oh, take me along," it shouts in glee,
As a meteor swaggers, "Come hang with me!"

With each passing black hole, it holds its breath,
Fascinated by the dance between life and death.
In the dark of space, it giggles with zest,
Who knew driftwood could be such a guest?

So, toast with a twig stuck on a star,
Celebrate moments both near and far.
In the cosmic ocean, we find our way,
Driftwood and laughter, come what may.

Paintings of Perception

I painted a star in a purple hue,
But it turned out brown with a dash of blue.
With each brushstroke, I laughed with delight,
As my canvas became a galactic sight.

The sun wore glasses, a quirky trend,
While the moon sighed, "Will this fashion end?"
Colors collided in a joyful spree,
Creating images only I could see.

A planet with arms did a jazzy dance,
Spinning and twirling, seizing its chance.
While asteroids chuckled, rolling along,
In a universe where all can belong.

So here's to the paintings that never stick,
To perceptions and truths that make us tick.
For in this mad gallery, joy is the theme,
Each color a note in a cosmic dream.

Abyssal Reveries

In the bottomless pit, a taco stand,
With nachos served by a floating hand.
Black holes offer salsa, spicy but nice,
And gravity's crunch adds the perfect spice.

Ghosts in the shadows play peek-a-boo,
While dark entities sip on cosmic brew.
"Who needs light?" they chuckle with cheer,
In this deep, endless void, there's nothing to fear.

A place where laughter and echoes unite,
Above ordinary, it feels just right.
With every giggle, the void starts to glow,
Remember, dear friend, it's all just for show.

In the abyss, where whimsy takes flight,
Dreams tumble and roll, a curious sight.
So join the jests in this boundless play,
For in all the darkness, let laughter sway.

Voices of the Abyss

In the void where echoes play,
Ghostly whispers roam all day.
Listen close to what they say,
Too much space? They went astray.

Banana peels drift on by,
In the dark, they often fly.
With a boom they bloop and pry,
A cosmic joke, oh me, oh my!

Bubbles burst in purple haze,
Dancing dust in silly ways.
They get lost in endless bays,
Comets spin in odd ballet.

Stars tune in, have a ball,
Giggling in their starlit hall.
Floating thoughts are big and small,
In the vastness, they enthrall.

Twilight's Embrace

A shadow lurks, it's time to prance,
With giggles in this midnight dance.
The moon winks, as if by chance,
Grinning at the night's romance.

Jelly beans swirl in the sky,
Candy comets whiz on by.
A chocolate sun, oh my, oh my,
Invites us all to give a try!

Whispers tickle with delight,
As wise old owls take their flight.
They joke about the stars' fright,
And steal the glow from fading light.

In twilight's charm, we laugh and play,
The cosmos joins in on the fray.
With stardust gleams and cosmic sway,
We find fun in night's display.

Wavelengths of the Unseen

Vibrations dance in empty air,
Whimsical tunes beyond compare.
Invisible notes float without a care,
Tickling ghosts, a spectral affair.

Jokes on frequencies we can't trace,
Dancing atoms pick up the pace.
They giggle as they twist and chase,
In wavelengths wide, they find their space.

Cereal boxes sing with glee,
Riding waves of mystery.
Banana boats sail endlessly,
Around the bends of what we see.

Laughter echoes, soft and bright,
In the night's warm, friendly light.
Even silence takes delight,
In the tunes of cosmic sight.

The Fabric of Night

Threads of shadow weave and twine,
In fabric dark, giggles combine.
Stars drop jokes from heights divine,
Knitting dreams in cosmic line.

A cat's meow causes a stir,
While shooting stars begin to purr.
Cotton candy clouds concur,
That nighttime mischief is a blur.

Lampshade moons peek through the seam,
Catching whispers in the dream.
A universe of laughter's beam,
Painting mischief's joyful theme.

Oh, what fun this night provides,
With giggles wrapped in cosmic rides.
In the fabric where joy collides,
The universe forever abides.

Void Serenades

In a vacuum, things float, just like my thoughts,
Drifting aimlessly, like lost sock knots.
Stars giggle at my unending chase,
Gravity check? Oh, what a wild race!

I tried to dance with an asteroid band,
But tripped on my tail—oh, wasn't it grand?
Space dust tickled my nose with a tease,
Chasing comets while I'm sneezing with ease.

Asteroids play games of hide and seek,
While supernovas laugh, giving me a peek.
Who knew the cosmos had such a flair?
With each swirl and twirl, they giggle in air!

So here's to the void, with laughter and cheer,
Where cosmic jesters toast with a beer.
Forget all your troubles, come take a ride,
In this hilarious space, where giggles collide!

Nebula Nocturnes

Floating clouds of gas, oh what a sight,
Making shapes like pancakes in the night.
I chuckled loudly, "Is that a cow?"
Or just another star changing its vow?

Twinkling lights dance like they're on a spree,
Just like me after too much soda tea.
Whirling through colors, cause who needs gray?
When swirling hues sing and sway!

Galactic friends call with sparkly phones,
"Join us for laughter, we've got cosmic tones!"
Supernova slapstick, oh what a scene,
As aliens burst forth, can you hear them scream?

So let's waltz through this colorful blast,
With jests and jests that are sure to last.
In this nebula, we'll laugh till we drop,
With cosmic giggles that never will stop!

Cosmic Lullabies

Twinkle, twinkle, little star,
Do you know how bizarre you are?
With winks and beams, you have a laugh,
Are you just playing with your own path?

Galaxies snore with a rumbly sound,
While clusters chuckle, all around.
"Dream of flying in this celestial space,
With aliens doing the funky face!"

Shooting stars wink as they zoom by,
"Here's a wish, just give it a try!"
Crickets on Mars sing a cheeky tune,
And even the comets have parties at noon!

As we lay under this nebula quilt,
We'll sway and giggle, hearts filled with guilt.
For missing out on all of this fun—
In the cradle of cosmos, we've only begun!

Celestial Echoes

Echoes of laughter bounce off the stars,
As planets giggle in their spinning cars.
Black holes are camping, roasting space s'mores,
While comets tell jokes, opening doors.

The Milky Way hosts a cosmic fair,
With rides that twist and bubble in air.
Aliens line up for the galactic spin,
With an ice cream sundae made of stardust within.

Quasars squeak and whirr in delight,
While meteors flash by, all in good sight.
"Whoops! That one slipped!" a starlet squawks,
As they all join in with goofy talks!

So here's to the echoes, the jests of the night,
In the vast vacuum, a festival of light.
With laughter resounding, let friendships soar,
In this cosmic playground, we always want more!

Eclipsed Rhythms

In the night, the stars play tricks,
Planets dance with cosmic flicks.
Galaxies in a silly race,
Wobbling in a clumsy space.

Comets laugh as they zoom past,
Chasing tails, a cosmic blast.
Nebulas with pastel hues,
Whisper secrets, giggle tunes.

Celestial Whispers

The moon spills jokes on the Earth,
Every glow, a giggling birth.
Saturn's rings, a jester's hat,
Twist and twirl like a playful cat.

Meteors sing songs out loud,
While shooting stars attract a crowd.
Cosmic dust with a wink and nod,
Creates smiles, it's all well trod.

Shadows of the Cosmos

In the void, shadows tease and play,
Twinkling lights lead them astray.
Black holes burp with a funny sound,
Sucking giggles from around.

Asteroids don't bump, they bounce,
Making friends with every pounce.
Meteor showers, oh what fun,
Splashing laughter, everyone!

Starlit Murmurs

Whispers echo through starry nights,
Bubbles pop with cosmic delights.
Galactic smiles stretch so wide,
As the universe enjoys the ride.

Constellations play hide and seek,
Nibbling light, they giggle and squeak.
Winking stars filled with glee,
Invite all to dance with me.

The Sound of Stars

Whispers float in cosmic air,
Stars giggle without a care.
Planets dance in silly spins,
While comets wear their brightest grins.

Asteroids play hide and seek,
In the silence, they all squeak.
Galaxies swirl in a waltz,
But black holes have the weirdest faults.

Nebulae splash in colors bright,
Making rainbows in the night.
Supernovae blast confetti,
While starlight twinkles, oh so petty.

Space's laughter never fades,
As laughter in the starlight wades.
In the vastness, joy's the key,
With cosmic jokes, we're all set free.

The Quiet of Infinity

In the hush of endless skies,
Wormholes giggle, oh how they rise!
Infinity wears a silly grin,
As galaxies spin round on a whim.

Cosmic dust tosses a wink,
While time just plays in the blink.
If you listen, you might just hear,
The universe crack up with cheer.

Black holes munch like they're in a feast,
Light tries to run, but it can't, at least.
The fabric of space is a joker's throne,
Stretching laughter till it's all blown.

So in this vast, quirky space,
Let's find joy in this embrace.
In the quiet, jokes abound,
In the cosmic chuckles, we are found.

Reflections in the Void

In the void where echoes play,
Reflections wink and often sway.
Mirrors flap like cosmic wings,
Making shadows of funny things.

Starlight giggles at the night,
While meteors soar in a flight.
The vacuum holds a merry tune,
As dark yawns wide like a cartoon.

When quasars hum their jolly song,
Even silence can't help but sing along.
The universe bursts with quirky flair,
With every bounce, it's joy we share.

Oh, the void is quite the jest,
With cosmic humor taking rest.
So let's dance in space's delight,
And laugh at stars, both day and night.

Celestial Solitude

In solitude where stardust roams,
Celestial jesters find their homes.
Gravity plays tricks on the cliff,
While the sun shares a playful riff.

Singularity wears a hat of glee,
As dimensional planes lounge carefree.
While moons toss jokes from afar,
Comets chuckle as they spar.

Meteor showers rain down giggles,
As planets whirl and twist with wiggles.
In solitude, stars like to play,
Making happiness the theme of the day.

So in this cosmic, quiet dance,
Laughter blooms, time takes a chance.
With every twinkle, a joke unfolds,
In celestial solitude, laughter holds.

Enigmatic Starlight

In shadows where the giggles roam,
Eager stars make jokes at home.
They twinkle and they play a prank,
On wandering minds, a cosmic tank.

A comet tripped on cosmic lace,
While planets laughed at space's pace.
The moon declared, 'I'm just a lamp!'
And silly suns danced like a champ.

Each twinkling wink, a mischievous tease,
As gravity trips like a breeze.
In this vastness, glee's the plot,
Where space and whispers fill the slot.

So raise a toast to stars that jive,
In wavelengths where the grin's alive.
For in the void, laughter's a thrill,
In beams unseen, we find the chill.

Whispers in the Abyss

Down in the depths, the echoes sing,
A jellyfish dons a crown of bling.
With seahorses tap-dancing away,
In this black sea, it's cabaret day.

Octopuses juggle with style and flair,
While mermaids giggle, flipping their hair.
In the abyss, the chatter's rife,
Coral reefs gossip like they're rife.

The anglerfish beams with a cheeky glow,
Saying, 'Who's the brightest? Come, see the show!'
A crab tells jokes, snappy and bright,
In murky depths, joy sparks the night.

Amidst the ink and shades of blue,
Listen close, hear the humor brew.
For in the deep, where shadows dwell,
Laughter bubbles, casting a spell.

Nightfall Reveries

When twilight paints the sky with glee,
And owls converse with bumblebees.
The stars in jammies start to play,
In dreaming realms where snickers stay.

The moon, a chef, stirs up delight,
With cosmic cookies served at night.
Shooting stars shoot pies from afar,
As night unfolds its joke bazaar.

Crickets hum a silly beat,
While fireflies dance on tiny feet.
The breeze carries laughter, light and free,
A serenade from the cosmic sea.

So lay back, let your dreams take flight,
In absurd tales of the starry night.
For in the dusk, where dreams convene,
Laughter reigns, forever keen.

Chasing Phantom Stars

In the chase for stars that giggle and twirl,
A flea asked a comet, 'Give it a whirl!'
He sprinted through wishes, absurd and bright,
With every wish, he leaped in delight.

Planets peeked with a wink and a grin,
As they spun in circles, inviting him in.
With playful halos, they crafted their charms,
While asteroids danced with open arms.

Each tail of stardust seemed to proclaim,
'Come join the fun, it's all just a game!'
So he flipped and he flopped through the velvety glow,
Chasing those phantoms, oh what a show!

Yet all were in jest, not one real spark,
Just shadows and giggles in the cosmic dark.
Still he laughed and he played, darting afar,
In the wild chase of the phantom star.

Starlit Silence

In the night where stars pop and fizz,
Cosmic confetti, a galactic whiz.
Aliens giggle, their laughter so sly,
Trying to dance in the milky way's pie.

Planets spin with a wobble and shake,
Asteroids chase like a runaway cake.
Comets trailing magic and light,
Who knew space could be such a sight?

Whispers of the Void

The void whispers jokes in a hush,
Black holes giggle in a cosmic rush.
They've got punchlines that make stars swoon,
While meteors tumble in an endless cartoon.

Galaxies twirl in a cosmic ballet,
Gravity's pull, the universe's sway.
Nebulas puff and then giggle a bit,
Creating a scene where the space critters sit.

Melodies of the Dark Sky

The dark sky croons a forgetful tune,
Choruses sung by the wayward moon.
Shooting stars strum on celestial strings,
As the laughter of quirks and quirks takes wing.

Zodiac critters play hide and seek,
While Saturn's rings give a twirl and a peek.
They share silly tales of space-time bends,
Where the wackiest universe never ends.

Twilight Harmonies

Twilight hums with a jazzy flair,
Shooting off beats through the cool night air.
Astro-beans frolic with gravity-free glee,
While comets slide in with a cosmic jubilee.

In the dusk, where starlight may tease,
Planets engage in a game of freeze.
They twinkle their secrets with a sly little grin,
In a universe filled with laughter within.

The Language of Shadows

Whispers of shadows dance and play,
Tickling the corners where sunlight can't stay.
They giggle and wiggle, making a mess,
In a world where the weird knows how to impress.

They speak in silence, a cheeky retort,
Playing tag in the dark, quite the sport!
Oh, how they frolic, those sneaky little sprites,
Turning our nightmares into delightful sights.

In the corners they hide, all jittery and spry,
Casting their jokes under the watchful sky.
With a flick and a swirl, they vanish from view,
Leaving us laughing at the things they construe.

So let's all embrace this whimsical tale,
Of playful shadows who never grow stale.
For in their chaotic, light-hearted spree,
Lies the joy of the night's own jubilee.

Ghosts of the Universe

Specters of space, in a swirling whirl,
Swapping their stories, giving time a twirl.
They hiccup in stardust, with laughter so bright,
Chasing away darkness, what a sight!

With a shiver and shake, they grab cosmic tea,
Chatting with comets, so jovially free.
In a dance of confusion, they glide and they spin,
Turning black holes into a ghostly grin.

Their ghoulish giggles echo through the void,
Painting the cosmos with mischief and joy.
Invisible antics, yet quite a display,
As they boogie across the Milky Way sway.

So look to the skies, where the phantoms frolic,
In a universe bursting with cheerful symbolic.
For every blink of a star may conceal,
A ghost that delights with a cosmic appeal.

Resonance of the Unknown

Bouncing beats of the unseen realm,
Twisting and turning, they're at the helm.
Echoes of laughter we've yet to hear,
Playing tag with shadows, drawing us near.

A riddle resounds in the echoes profound,
Tickling our senses with joy unbound.
With whispers of nonsense and quirky refrains,
They jive in the silence, where mischief remains.

Through the giggles of galaxies, wonders abound,
A chorus of candor dances all around.
As we ponder the beats of the cosmic unknown,
We join in the revelry, never alone.

So raise a toast to the quirks we can't see,
To the mysteries hidden, a jolly jubilee.
For in every silence, there's laughter profound,
In the resonance of life, we joyously drown.

Stars Beyond Sight

In twinkling trails, there are secrets untold,
Stars that play games, both silly and bold.
Hiding in shadows, they make quite a fuss,
In a cosmos of chaos, creating a bus!

They wink with delight, oh what a jest,
Giggling through blackness, they never rest.
With each shooting star, a prank in the night,
Reminding us all to keep laughter in sight.

So let's count the stars and embrace the spree,
Of light-hearted banter in the galaxy.
For beyond our vision, they frolic and glide,
In a universe bustling with silliness applied.

So next time you gaze at the heavens so wide,
Remember the laughter that joyfully hides.
In the depths of the cosmos, the mirth does ignite,
With stars beyond sight bringing pure delight.

www.ingramcontent.com/pod-product-compliance
Lightning Source LLC
Chambersburg PA
CBHW051642160426
43209CB00004B/758